The Mirror of Life

Sayontan Ghosh

BookLeaf
Publishing

The Mirror of Life © 2022 Sayontan Ghosh

All rights reserved.

No part of this publication may be reproduced, stored in a retrieval system, or transmitted, in any form or by any means, electronic, mechanical, photocopying, recording or otherwise, without the prior written permission of the presenters.

Sayontan Ghosh asserts the moral right to be identified as author of this work.

Presentation by *BookLeaf Publishing*

Web: www.bookleafpub.com

E-mail: info@bookleafpub.com

ISBN: 978-93-95413-33-6

First edition 2022

DEDICATION

This book is dedicated to my father, mother, sister, brother-in-law, and most importantly to YOU! Also to myself.

ACKNOWLEDGEMENT

Firstly, I would like to express my heartfelt gratitude and love for my parents who have believed in me throughout, no matter what. I would also like to express my love and gratitude to my sister and brother-in-law who have instilled in me a sense of independence and believed that I am meant to achieve great heights in all aspects of my life.

I express my deepest gratitude to Irin, who asked me to pick up the pen to write again. Without her convincing me to write again, this book would not be possible. I would also take the time to thank my friends Tushar, Siddharth, Armaan, and Yash who have helped me out in more ways than one.

PREFACE

The Mirror of Life has been born out of inspiration, perspiration, tears, sweat, glory, and most importantly, perspective. It is a narration of events that has happened in lives of people with my eyes and my attempt at re-tellability of the same events. I would like to take this opportunity to express my deepest gratitude to my parents, sister, and brother-in-law who have believed in me and have strived to make me a person capable of achieving things which I didn't believe was true earlier. I would also like to take the time to express my gratitude to my dear friend Irin, who helped me to start writing again after I was in a slump for the last two to three years. It is because of the belief my support system has had in me for all these years, I have picked up the pen to write and am using these words to speak.

These writings have always been in my thoughts, emotions, feelings, and I am expressing them. It is a way of reaching out to you, to tell you, you are not alone going through the things that you are going through. I am also there. I just happen to be the writer, you happen to be the reader. In a few cases, it might be opposite. Most of the experiences are fictional or personal and hence, the book was named accordingly.

The biggest challenge for me, personally, was to get back to writing. I had stopped writing for the last two to three years, because of several reasons and one of the biggest reasons was probably that I was going through depression. This book has provided me with inspiration to start writing again, to express myself again, and to live again. To live in an unapologetic manner and that's precisely why I am writing this book. The purpose of this book to give you hope that you will come across something tomorrow that will make your life a lot more meaningful, than however meaningful it has been till today.

An evening to Remember

Lying next to each other,
We watched Palm Springs,
Put on a blanket and Netflix,
Beautiful calm beings,
Some chips to taste,
Some time to waste,
We watched stars,
Heard birds and cars,
Some iced tea cooled us down,
Passion warmed us up,
We lost ourselves in each other,
And we ended up getting a bit more found.

No good in goodbyes

I got tears in my eyes,
I got tears in my smile,
I got tears, I don't know why,
I don't, I don't try,
Tears don't fall, I don't cry,
Take a bullet for my Valentine,
I don't die, can't say goodbye,
Goodbyes aren't good, so why,
Do we call it a goodbye?
If anything, it's a good lie,
And it's a good try to try and hide,
The feelings behind a goodbye

Outstretched

The muscles are outstretched,
Dreams are farfetched,
But, they are etched, in my skin,
In my mind, it's sketched,
Living on the edge,
Knowing the ledge,
Paying homage,
When I write on every page.

Shooting Stars

He won't accept the cut,
The actor is too tired,
And butt hurt,
He feels stuck in a rut,
The shot takes forever,
It's boring now,
Wants to say never,
But his mouth is shut,
Coz this involves paper.

Empty Thoughts

5

Just going to thank, being empty,
Point blank, Tabula Rasa,
Page left blank,
Empty thoughts,
I got empty thoughts in think tank,

Ink doesn't spill, From the quill,
Time stands still, Guess I need a refill,
Oh! This page is already filled.

"You" & "I"

Where does "I" stop?

Is it when eyes drop?

Or when eye drops,

Fall on these eyes,

Like ice blocks ?

To me, it was you,

To you, I was "You",

Similar but different views,

Still similar to "You".

Desires burn in more ways than one

Always wanted a son,
Didn't get one, Life plays in different ways,
Had it's own fun,
Now, it's a U turn,

Daughter's getting married,
He gets to learn,
She doesn't want sons.

Acid Attack Survivor

They threw acid on my face,
Now, I'm a public disgrace ?
Isn't it funny ? The irony ?
I'm the victim and they accuse me of tyranny!

Welcome Home

Hey stranger,

It was nice to know you,
Then, I got to know you,
A little bit more,
And you were no longer,
A stranger, like before,
And, if all doors,
Shut on you,
I'll hold my door,
Welcome to home.

Hungry & Content

Get more than you ask.

Ask more than you get,

Don't lose heart,

Breathe in your chest,

Life's got a test ?

This is a fun fest.

Fears have to rest,

As courage is exercised,

By those who are blessed.

The voices make a lot of noise

Air, want to breathe in,

A turmoil within,

Heart's beating, Mind's tripping,

Voices are gripping,

When I'm awake,

They're sleeping,

But when they're awake,

I stop breathing.

Adulting is ...

World's blowing up,

People growing up

Adulthood,

Got kids throwing up,

Some still up,

Some not showing up,

Like river and rapids,

Still going rough

Music is here

Blast songs in my ear,
Praying I can disappear,
In a different dimension,
Out of the atmosphere,

Close my eyes,
Open my ears,
The noise is gone,
Music is here.

Past/Present/Future.

The changes of the past,

Still lurk,

Shadows cast,

But, change is a constant,

So will it last? Or will it go so fast?

As I ask,

Is the past so vast,

That I'm still rolling in it?

That's all I ask.

Stop Terrorism

The ground is slipping,

The world is flipping,

All going for the thug life,

Everyone's killing,

They carry arms,

For their protection, Like all want to harm,

Look at the ego!

It's perfection.

Beautiful Strangers

I met someone yesterday,

Blew my mind away,

She's gone, Her memories stay,

She gave food to eat,

She gave water to drink,

To a homeless person,

Without giving a blink.

The saint who played peasant

I met him once, He dressed like a peasant,
Collecting alms, Extremely calm and pleasant,
And my mind wondered about his presence
Then, I got to know,
He played saint,
Giving hope to pained,
Leaving their brains
Questioning in his effervescence.

Thankful for Today

Turn over a new leaf,

Get a belief,

Make that belief,

Make you believe,

Even though yesterday,

you in grief,

Today's here,
Feel relieved.

www.ingramcontent.com/pod-product-compliance
Lightning Source LLC
Chambersburg PA
CBHW070731160726
48003CB00006BA/2450